the 7-hour experiment

a personal journey into the self

s a n d y   w e a t h e r a l l

acknowledgements

This is dedicated to all of my teachers and inspirations. Most of them do not realize they have had this role in my life.

I want to thank the teachers I have never met. Gabby Bernstein taught me that the Universe Has My Back (and just when I needed it, as she says often happens). Dr. Joe Dispenza taught me I can change my reality, Michael Singer is still teaching me to surrender, and Eckhart Tolle reminds me to be present.

I want to thank Sara Cueva for teaching me to love myself through yoga, and the "Lisas" who guided me in body and spirit. My fellow yogis of the "Hell Yeah" Tribe who accepted and embraced me.

Mom and Dad. Because I'm here. Dad, I'm so grateful we found our way. I love you both.

To my Facebook friends—yes, Facebook friends! Thanks to those who have read my words and said, "You should write a book!" or told me my words made a difference for them. You gave me courage.

Kelly Wolf, you keep reminding me of my yellow light. Thank you for believing in my writing and my energy.

Gary Whyte. Thanks for your wise guidance in editing. You have mentored me more than you know. Photography, words and life stuff.

Tasha Benscoter. For helping me figure out design and for being that person who is just easy to talk to.

Balboa Press and Hay House. For getting this thing out there.

Kevin
ho'oponopono

White Temple, Chiang Rai, Thailand

Balboa Press books may be ordered through booksellers or by contacting:

Balboa Press

A Division of Hay House

1663 Liberty Drive

Bloomington, IN 47403

www.balboapress.com

1 (877) 407-4847

Because of the dynamic nature of the Internet, any web addresses or links contained in this book may have changed since publication and may no longer be valid. The views expressed in this work are solely those of the author and do not necessarily reflect the views of the publisher, and the publisher hereby disclaims any responsibility for them.

The author of this book does not dispense medical advice or prescribe the use of any technique as a form of treatment for physical, emotional, or medical problems without the advice of a physician, either directly or indirectly. The intent of the author is only to offer information of a general nature to help you in your quest for emotional and spiritual well-being. In the event you use any of the information in this book for yourself, which is your constitutional right, the author and the publisher assume no responsibility for your actions.

ISBN: 978-1-9822-2470-7 (sc)

ISBN: 978-1-9822-2471-4 (e)

Print information available on the last page.

Balboa Press rev. date: 05/23/2019

an introduction

If I write a book now, I'm full of shit! Right?

People who write books have already woken up. They have it figured out. But not me. Somedays, some things make so much sense, and then other days, I'm still so confused. As I write this today, I am confused.

But I've heard, "You're supposed to write a book." So what am I supposed to write about? Do I write about all of this confusion? How some of us just have to keep figuring it out as we go? Or do I talk about how we want to scream in the night because we're afraid? Or the feeling that we have no voice because we're expected to have a certain demeanour and act in a certain way? Or maybe write about those of us who are aware of what we're supposed to do but, even with all the tools in our belts, still don't seem to be able to get it quite right? Or am I supposed to write about what it's like to be human — and not awake?

I think one of the most painful things can be to have the desire to wake up; knowing what we have to do to move toward fulfilling that desire, and yet not being able to do it. So what is the secret to answering this question? At this very moment, I literally feel paralyzed; afraid to take the next step.

But I won't turn to food or alcohol or drugs. I won't use sex or gambling or shopping. I won't numb with Netflix or over-exercising or too much social media. I won't go to extremes of cold or hot; of deprivation or stimulation. I won't use extreme sports or more zen.

I will look this fear in the eye and say, "I see you." I see you and I will watch you. I will notice the voice in my head and not resist — not talk back. I will look after my body. I will look after my mind. I will look after my spirit. I will listen to my heart and trust my intuition.

I will not be influenced by every word from every other person, thinking they know what's better for me. I haven't trusted myself before, so when someone has told me I should "do this or that," I have thought that maybe they were right. So I follow another podcast or hold another crystal in my hand or use a different toothpaste or read a different book. All good things if they are authentic to the advisor; but does that mean they are good for me? I don't know, because I haven't really trusted or listened to what is right for me. And if I feel brave enough to express what is working for me and then hear another doubt so that I judge or question myself for a second, I lose my faith in it.

But when I ask myself, "Who am I?" I don't get those kinds of answers. I am not told to do or try, to be something else or someone else. I hear, "Be nothing, no one, no identity. Be."

Don't even try.

Go back to bed.

Sleep for an hour.

Let the cortisol chemicals leave your body.

Wake up.

Feed the cats.

Eat.

Shower.

Start your list.

Feel at peace.

Trust you know.

It will be as it should.

You will be held.

You will be guided.

You will be loved.

the decision

Upon waking at my second alarm, about 7 AM, I sat upright in bed to meditate. I vaguely remembered the previous intention that I had typed in my phone. But I did not recognize the passion in it until I re-read it just now.

I sat to meditate, a throw blanket over my head because I was so cold. I sat draped like a ghost. I felt like a ghost. In that very moment, instead of meditating, I came up with this experiment. I have never had such an idea cross my mind before: to take seven hours to ask a single question. I did not even consciously choose seven hours. I just knew I would start around 8 AM, and that as much as I wanted to do nothing else, at 3 PM I should get back to life. Practice yoga. Do some work. So I set my alarm and put my phone away. Not once did I check it. I listened, even though I thought it **as** strange as some of you might be thinking. I didn't even know why I should do this — just that I should. I also had no expectations for what it meant. I knew though, that I needed to ask,

"Who am I?"

This is a question of ancient yogic practice. Something to meditate on. The day before, it came to me, re-reading *The Untethered Soul* by Michael Singer. That same day I was listening to Oprah's "SuperSoul Conversations" with Eckhart Tolle, and once again the "Who am I?" crossed my awareness. So I awoke this morning, had breakfast, fed the cats. I did not shower or get out of my robe. I grabbed my meditation cushion, my blankets. Picked a spot on the floor outside the closet — and began to sit.

For the entire seven hours, each time I stopped to write I had no idea what time it was nor for how long I had been "gone." So as you read, perhaps an hour passed between entries. Perhaps ten minutes. I would write, then regroup, maybe move to a different spot in my room on the floor — always on the floor; sitting, sometimes lying down. And then begin again.

Everything you read is as it was written in a semi-conscious state. Or perhaps a little more conscious.

San Pedro, Belize

seated in the self

Here is my experiment.

I am shutting off until 3 PM today.

No phone.

No computer.

No food.

Only bathroom. Water.

Cats are fed.

I have nowhere to be. No one will even be wondering about me today.

So I will sit until I know who I am.

I grabbed the journal intuitively — even though not my original intention. Already the thoughts came that I think will matter enough to write down.

I kept asking who I am and instead I began to think of others and who they were. How can I possibly know others when I don't even know who I am? But it's easier to try and figure out others because then we don't have to know ourselves. And when we are really having a problem with self is when we spend more time defining others — labelling even. Name calling at our lowest vibration — even if it's only in our heads, but sometimes to others who will listen to us. We make up things about others we know less about than we know ourselves. We project that which we are. If we feel like others are blaming us, it's probably because we are blaming. If we are feeling judged, it's probably because we are judging.

If we are feeling controlled, it's probably because we are trying to control. I learned about this projection in therapy. It's psychology. It's been observed and researched. It's what I call holding up the ugly mirror. That which we feel is most done to us, is likely what we are most doing to others.

So if at this moment I am feeling a little rejected, it's probably because I have been rejecting.

Ahh. Ouch.

excuses

(I wrote this in large caps because my early entries were written only by the hint of light that my eyes could adjust to. I'm only aware of my thought process here being about how others could also do this experiment if they didn't have my luxury of freelance)

PHONE IN EXISTENTIAL CRISIS

HEAVILY MEDITATED

CONSCIOUSNESS LEAVE

clockwise (from upper left): Hopkins, Belize Old City Wall, Chiang Mai, Thailand; Grand Palace, Bangkok, Thailand

wholeness

What does it mean when we say we don't feel whole?

How is it even possible?

We say we have lost a part of ourselves when we lose a relationship or through the separation of death. How? How?!

Our bodies have not been divided into parts. I don't think our souls can be compartmentalized and chunks given away or taken from us. It's impossible. We cannot be divided this way. So how can we lose ourselves?

We can lose another but not ourselves. Yet I don't think we ever really lose another. *We will always be energetically connected to everyone we encounter and especially to those with whom we have had a deeper connection.*

What about when we say we gave ourselves away to another? But what have we given away? Our dignity? Our power? Our light? Not possible. Once again, we cannot be divided from ourselves. If we cannot be divided, how can we give ourselves away?

We were born whole. We grew up whole. Even if we had trauma or challenges or difficult relationships we did not give pieces of ourselves away. Not possible.

Are we missing a limb and another person has it now? Could our heart beat if we gave a chunk away? And our souls—our souls! I don't know how you picture a soul, but I imagine a continuous orb of light. Light cannot be separated like that. It's fluid. Does it appear fragmented in your vision?

Think about this.

How can you NOT be whole? You are whole. I am whole. No matter what.

Sunset Boulevard, Los Angeles

know ourselves

How can we be
in wholeness with
another unless we
know who we are?

Sunset Boulevard, Los Angeles (L); Xunantunich Mayan Ruin, Belize (R)

sensation

I just feel a sensation now.

I just feel cold.

I need a blanket.

I came back to body simply because I was cold.

I can't quite identify with me though.

Strange. I just noticed I labelled this.

My legs are also numb. Maybe that's why I am cold.

Or maybe my legs are numb because I am cold.

I don't know the time. I will not check but I think I have many hours yet.

I already want to lie down but I will sit longer with another blanket.

fear

I fell asleep.

And now I'm afraid to wake up. Literally and figuratively.

I realize there is some fear to becoming awake. I never knew this before. I always thought I would embrace the journey to waking up; the most beautiful thing.

But waking up means saying goodbye to the constructed self. Saying my goodbyes to everything I feel I know to be true; but I know are not true.

I'm also afraid that I *won't* wake up, which is probably even *more* frightening.

It is the loss that makes me afraid. I have already lost relationships. I lost what I felt was my most important relationship. I feel some friendships slipping away. Growth often creates conflict. Change is here for us. Even good change can create anger and resentment. I know my change has been good but how I handled some of the speed bumps along the way has been less than smooth.

The honesty here is stinging me.

Why is this work today so important?

I made the decision to do this because I felt I had hit rock bottom this weekend. I have hit the bottom before and almost died. My bottom is higher now. No eating disorder. No TV *(not that TV is bad—I just no longer use it to tune out)*. I did drink one night and that was a sign to me that I never want to go back there.

The feeling of aloneness is a reminder of my last bottom. *Note: I didn't say loneliness—I think there is a difference and I actually like when I see the word "aloneness." It defines the physical of being alone but not the emotional feeling of loneliness.*

I don't want to go to the past. This is a higher bottom but it's still low enough to know that I have to make these changes.

I have no idea what time it is or how long I have been asleep. I resist the urge to check.

I will go to the bathroom and quench my thirst and even put on clothes and then sit once more.

previous spread: White Temple, Chiang Rai, Thailand

San Pedro, Belize

what am I doing?

I've never been to a retreat, so I'm speculating here, but during my break before I sit again, I come to realize that this *may* be like going to a retreat. A dedicated time and space to do this work, to be aware; except I'm alone in my room, in my house.

I have this urge to get back to work, to be productive, as though my world could fall apart in the next seven hours because I'm postponing the things I should be doing. I say *should*. I should get that photography contract back. I should paint. I should workout. And yet none of these things will stop the world from turning. It will go on without me doing any of them. Not a soul will notice my experiment— even if I don't answer the phone or an email. No one is checking in on me. A little sad but it's not that important.

This time, this experiment, is the most important thing I can do. I had different plans for this day but when I had the cortisol running through my body at 5 AM, something that has not affected me for a very long time, I knew this was the most important thing for me to do.

I chose to go back to sleep to release the cortisol. When my next alarm went off, I realized I felt as if I had been told to do this experiment. The timing is perfect. Nobody at home. Nobody having any immediate expectations of me. Nobody expecting anything from me generally, anymore. One of the liberations of lost relationships. Nobody expects anything of you. Only in intimacy do the expectations run high. From both sides. *Don't kid yourself.* Lovers, friends, family.

You can tell from my words how far I am from awakening. I am still stuck in ego. *But at least I can give myself credit for noticing!*

Now I sit.

Ubud, Bali (top); Hopkins, Belize (bottom)

the power to choose

I only want to write briefly because I want to go back. Earlier, I had self-admitted to being in a depressive state. Old neural pathways began to creep in. REALLY OLD ones. Ones I had worked through in therapy. Fear, too. All the losses. And what about the future? Who will I love? Who will love me? Is anyone thinking of me now? Writing these words has the potential to put me back in that state but instead—I am *joyful*, even *blissful*.

I did that. Who? Me. That's all I know. I don't know who "Me" is except it's who I've always been. Not Sandy. Not an artist. Not a friend. Not a woman. Just Me.

And I made this happen.

Physically touching my heart makes a difference. There is science to back it up. I imagined my future life as if it had already happened. I even saw my last love and me together again but honest, authentic and happy. I know it might not be him, but I felt real love and gratitude. I also saw me helping people through the books I write. Yes, books. I see books now. I saw my house and my red Toyota 4 Runner. Stuff still, yes, but the most profound thing is that I shifted my state. In fact, before I visualized my future, touching my heart, I began to choose joy, then bliss. THEN, I was able to visualize. When the state or vibration is low, it's hard to visualize because you don't believe it. So we must first change our state. Otherwise, we're still relying on the external—even the imaginary external—to make a difference.

I did this! I changed my state. I want to open the curtains now. I want to go outside. I want to celebrate this, but I also want to go back.

I still don't know what time it is. I feel hunger, but I have an idea. By not tuning into the normal patterns, I will change my pathways.

No high expectations for this experiment. It must be sustainable, but I know I am rewiring my brain in all of these moments. I don't expect. *I know!* I am certain. I have created a positive shift already. I know that by the time my alarm rings later today, I will be different.

I will have changed my life.

All the noise from the last entry, the "negative" emotions, judgements toward self or others, have gone. And I now will put "negative" in quotations, because with all the work I have done I no longer believe in labelling emotions as negative or positive—they are just aspects of how we manifest those emotions.

I still don't know who I am, and I certainly still can't think I know others.

Allow. Allow. Allow.

With joy.

Let's go back now. Hmm … who is this "let's" I speak of. Curious.

Hopkins, Belize (top); Hopkins, Belize (bottom)

two possibilities

I wanted to go right back but then thoughts appeared. I think of Michael Singer who talks about thoughts not being controllable, and so I let them come without judgement. I realize that some of what I am exploring is influenced by Dr. Joe Dispenza and Gregg Braden (host of GAIA TV's "Missing LInks" series) and the quantum physics model. They teach us that we can change our thoughts and by doing so change our energy and on a quantum level create entirely new lives.

Yet Michael Singer's marvellous theory (as I interpret it) says that our existence doesn't influence the Universe. The Universe has been and always will be, regardless of our thoughts, and our only purpose is to just let go. In letting go we create entirely new lives.

Are they conflicting? Not really, because this soup is making sense of another understanding for me. I think both theories apply.

I JUST NOW made this connection.

For some reason, I am reminded of Forrest Gump.

As Forrest Gump said: "I don't know if Momma was right or if, if it's Lieutenant Dan. I don't know if we each have a destiny, or if we're all just floating around accidental-like on a breeze, but I, I think maybe it's both. Maybe both are happening at the same time."

Maybe we surrender and create.

We exist independent of the Universe. It will always BE without us, but we also experience and observe. By doing so, we are co-creators of the Universe that goes on without us. A little mind blowing as I write this but it makes sense.

I am imagining the mites on my skin eating the dead cells, and from the cells to the molecules to the atoms. Then this body away and my energy expanding to create new DNA strands simply from my joy, so this DNA changes. My biology changes. My energy changes. That energy is going out to the Universe now, even though it seems I am just this small being in a confined space. But it expands. I know it expands because I feel expansive.

Even if one photon of energy can reach another in an elevated state, is it possible for this to affect change?

I want to ask these questions even though I don't even know if "my science" is sensical. I kind of feel like I'm making shit up, but then isn't that, in itself, fascinating? That this energetic being can create worlds and ideas out of all the input that comes in? It is why I want more input. I want to learn.

How can this desire be anything but a miracle?

In just a few short hours following my morning decision, to just sit today, I have come from a cortisol-ridden body to a creative state.

I'm going back in now!

What's coming?

No expectations.

I may have hit the peak (for today).

But Damn!

overleaf: Grand Palace, Bangkok, Thailand

ego. full on

Just realized I'm doing something I have NEVER done before.

No wonder I was afraid. I can see others being afraid of this. It seems rather benign in the big picture—but it is not.

Even ignoring technology (and time). Wow!

What's this now?

Ego arises—reminding me that it's here to create suffering.

I just had thoughts, pains, anger, feelings of betrayal.

My first omission. Work yet to be done.

But I made a change a while ago.

I still don't know how much time has passed. I'm going to open the curtains. Move toward waking. Find some sun and sit again.

Venice Beach, California

San Pedro, Belize

knowing of
an infant

The ego created the last for sure; wants
the pain to come back. That's its job.

I ask the ego to go, and once again ask,

"Who am I?"

I'm lying on the floor. The sun
streaming in. I'm allowing whatever
comes, to come.

I see all of the babies in the city now.
Those lying in cribs. Not wondering
who they are because they already
know. I return to this. The knowing of
an infant.

Hopkins, Belize

separation

I almost feel like I'm running out of time. The ego curveball created some fear. I have been thinking of my therapy. Should I go back to it? Or am I *really* changing my brain? I believed I was. The ego created doubt. The ego is a powerful thing but not as powerful as "Me."

I am cold here.

I want to quit this experiment. I still don't know what time it is, even with the sun shining. How strange it is to have no time. No technology. No connection, yet surrounded by the city.

I am starting to realize how strange I am. I don't feel like I fit with the hippy crowd totally. I don't fit with the conservatives. I don't fit with the scientists. I don't fit with the artists. I don't even fit with the fringes.

But that thought creates separation. And yet, because of this experiment I actually feel more connected. Once again, I recognize I was thinking with ego—not truth.

Who Am I?

I am starting to see the strangeness in me. And it's OK.

Who else wakes up one morning and makes this an experiment for the day?

Grand Palace, Bangkok, Thailand (L); Tribal Village, Chiang Rai, Thailand (R)

White Temple, Chiang Rai, Thailand (top); White Temple, Chiang Rai, Thailand (bottom)

love

This time, as soon as I sat upright and closed my eyes, the cat meowed. Then I felt surrounded by energy and I knew it was God.

You may have a definition of God that suits, but I don't know that I have a clear definition of it as yet. In fact, I only started reintroducing the word God into my vocabulary and my thoughts because, for years, the God I was taught to believe in didn't make sense to me. But I cannot find another way to describe it.

God is not an entity but an energy. Bigger than us, but maybe it is the collective of all of us, of all our energies.

I'm not a religious person. I even hesitate to use the term spiritual person. My own opinion is that once we label ourselves in this way, it is just another form of ego. Once again, Eckhart Tolle describes this idea of how the ego acts.

Love. Love, even though I am strange (Ha). Love. Unconditional love.

I didn't want to stop this feeling to write, but I was promised I would get it back.

I must record this journey today.

who am I?

Who am I?

I was just about to write, but I still don't know the time.

I don't believe it's a coincidence that the three o'clock alarm sounded just as I was thinking what I now know are my last thoughts.

Who am I?

I am me.

I am me before I met the new people yesterday.

I am me before I met any of the friends I know, from my most recent yoga friends, to my skydiver friends, to my friends from over 20 years ago, to my earliest friends such as Brent, who I have known since I was four years old.

I am me before I met my last love.

I am me before I was aware of my siblings.

I am me before I was aware of my parents.

I am me before my experience in the womb.

But most importantly, I am me before I was incarnated into this life.

I just spent seven hours alone in silence. In meditation, other than when I was writing. I'm not even sure I was in deep, but considering I spent seven hours not really knowing or being aware if I was actually aware, I probably was.

Am I relieved to be done? A little. A little sad, even. I have thought occasionally what it must be like for those forced into solitude.

I *chose* to do this.

I think it was worth it.

Bangkok, Thailand

conclusion

Two days later, as I read that last sentence, I begin to wonder what was the point of this? I changed many things in myself but many are still the same and still require work.

I said I had no expectations but I guess that's not entirely true. I didn't have any at the time of the experiment, but today I wish that I had one of those defining moments experienced by some of the great teachers, like Eckhart Tolle, who kind of just "woke up."

But then I think of the Buddha; Siddhartha more precisely. Siddhartha did not just wake up one day. He spent years on his path of discovery, searching for several years before his moment under the Bodhi tree.

So here is my lesson to myself and to share.

For most of us, it is going to take time, awareness and forgiveness. My experiment taught me to explore, let go of expectations and receive joy and love when it comes.

My experiment taught me to notice ego when it comes and then release it to find freedom.

My experiment taught me that it's not just okay to be human, but that being human is to be beautiful, rich and varied.

My experiment taught me that doing something different than we have done before will make a difference.

My experiment taught me that even in solitude and silence we are all connected.

My experiment reminded me that our heart is the seat of the soul.

My experiment reminded me to always keep an open heart and to always …

Lead with Love.

Bangkok, Thailand

the photographs

| 2 |  | **White Temple, Chiang Rai, Thailand** — I ended up in Chiang Rai by accident. I had visa issues trying to get into Vietnam and so I had to regroup. I almost panicked but then decided to see Chiang Rai; the highlight stop of Thailand for me. The White Temple is a spectacular piece of contemporary art and spiritual solace. The most "natural" space was the representation of The Buddha at his time of awakening under the Bodhi tree. Few of the swarms of tourists stopped by this quiet spot for its lack of the spectacular. I stopped, meditated briefly, and moved on |

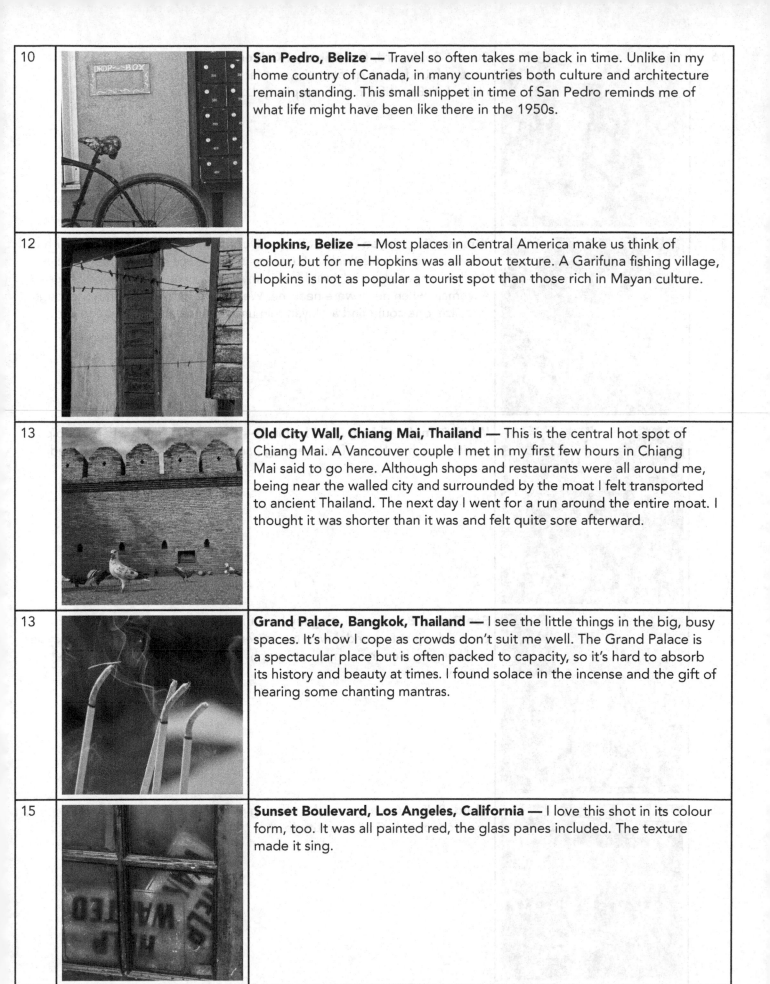

10		**San Pedro, Belize** — Travel so often takes me back in time. Unlike in my home country of Canada, in many countries both culture and architecture remain standing. This small snippet in time of San Pedro reminds me of what life might have been like there in the 1950s.
12		**Hopkins, Belize** — Most places in Central America make us think of colour, but for me Hopkins was all about texture. A Garifuna fishing village, Hopkins is not as popular a tourist spot than those rich in Mayan culture.
13		**Old City Wall, Chiang Mai, Thailand** — This is the central hot spot of Chiang Mai. A Vancouver couple I met in my first few hours in Chiang Mai said to go here. Although shops and restaurants were all around me, being near the walled city and surrounded by the moat I felt transported to ancient Thailand. The next day I went for a run around the entire moat. I thought it was shorter than it was and felt quite sore afterward.
13		**Grand Palace, Bangkok, Thailand** — I see the little things in the big, busy spaces. It's how I cope as crowds don't suit me well. The Grand Palace is a spectacular place but is often packed to capacity, so it's hard to absorb its history and beauty at times. I found solace in the incense and the gift of hearing some chanting mantras.
15		**Sunset Boulevard, Los Angeles, California** — I love this shot in its colour form, too. It was all painted red, the glass panes included. The texture made it sing.

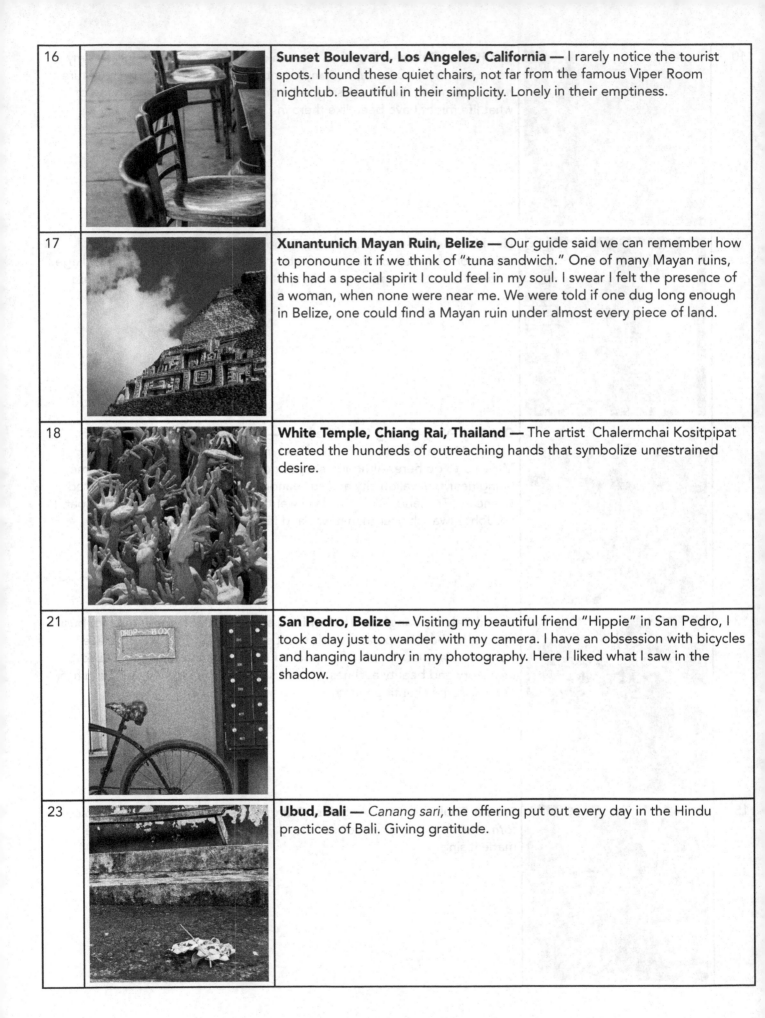

| 16 | | **Sunset Boulevard, Los Angeles, California —** I rarely notice the tourist spots. I found these quiet chairs, not far from the famous Viper Room nightclub. Beautiful in their simplicity. Lonely in their emptiness. |

| 17 | | **Xunantunich Mayan Ruin, Belize —** Our guide said we can remember how to pronounce it if we think of "tuna sandwich." One of many Mayan ruins, this had a special spirit I could feel in my soul. I swear I felt the presence of a woman, when none were near me. We were told if one dug long enough in Belize, one could find a Mayan ruin under almost every piece of land. |

| 18 | | **White Temple, Chiang Rai, Thailand —** The artist Chalermchai Kositpipat created the hundreds of outreaching hands that symbolize unrestrained desire. |

| 21 | | **San Pedro, Belize —** Visiting my beautiful friend "Hippie" in San Pedro, I took a day just to wander with my camera. I have an obsession with bicycles and hanging laundry in my photography. Here I liked what I saw in the shadow. |

| 23 | | **Ubud, Bali —** *Canang sari*, the offering put out every day in the Hindu practices of Bali. Giving gratitude. |

23	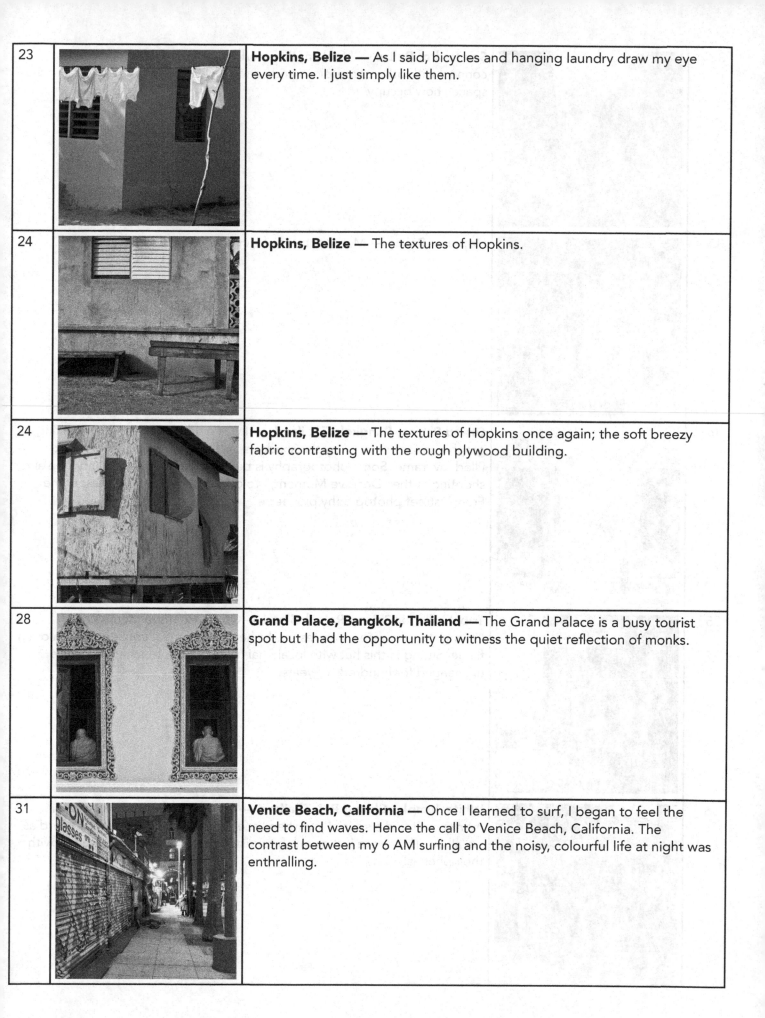	**Hopkins, Belize** — As I said, bicycles and hanging laundry draw my eye every time. I just simply like them.
24		**Hopkins, Belize** — The textures of Hopkins.
24		**Hopkins, Belize** — The textures of Hopkins once again; the soft breezy fabric contrasting with the rough plywood building.
28		**Grand Palace, Bangkok, Thailand** — The Grand Palace is a busy tourist spot but I had the opportunity to witness the quiet reflection of monks.
31		**Venice Beach, California** — Once I learned to surf, I began to feel the need to find waves. Hence the call to Venice Beach, California. The contrast between my 6 AM surfing and the noisy, colourful life at night was enthralling.

32	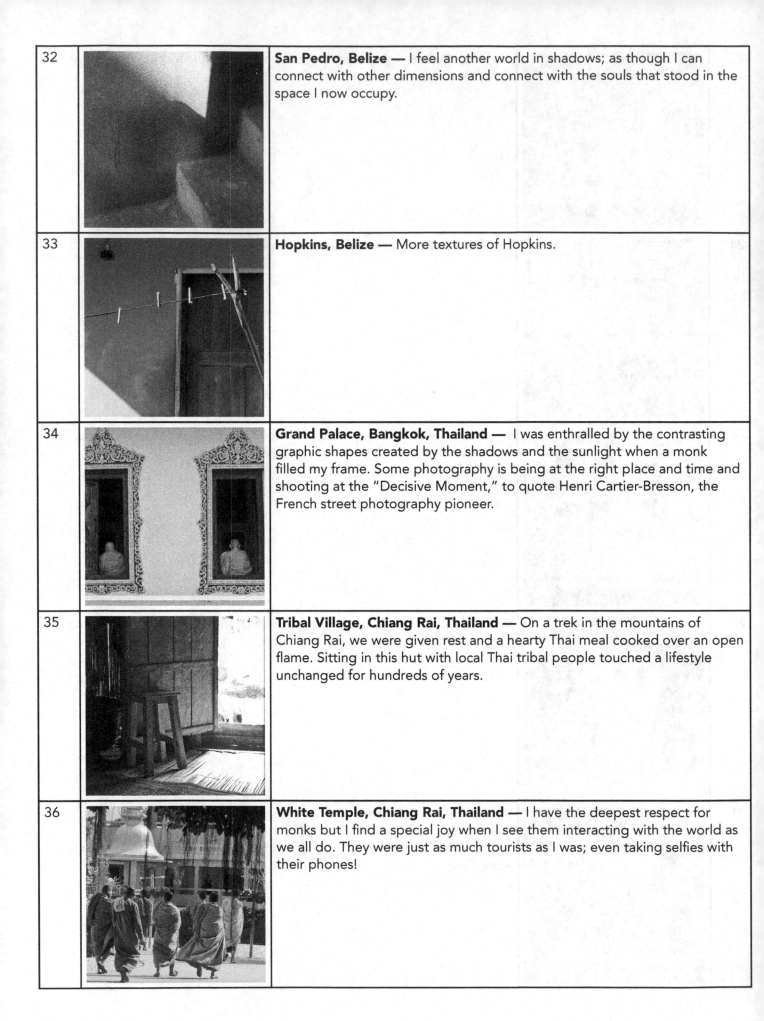	**San Pedro, Belize —** I feel another world in shadows; as though I can connect with other dimensions and connect with the souls that stood in the space I now occupy.
33		**Hopkins, Belize —** More textures of Hopkins.
34		**Grand Palace, Bangkok, Thailand —** I was enthralled by the contrasting graphic shapes created by the shadows and the sunlight when a monk filled my frame. Some photography is being at the right place and time and shooting at the "Decisive Moment," to quote Henri Cartier-Bresson, the French street photography pioneer.
35		**Tribal Village, Chiang Rai, Thailand —** On a trek in the mountains of Chiang Rai, we were given rest and a hearty Thai meal cooked over an open flame. Sitting in this hut with local Thai tribal people touched a lifestyle unchanged for hundreds of years.
36		**White Temple, Chiang Rai, Thailand —** I have the deepest respect for monks but I find a special joy when I see them interacting with the world as we all do. They were just as much tourists as I was; even taking selfies with their phones!

36		**White Temple, Chiang Rai, Thailand** — The intricate, fascinating artwork of Chalermchai Kositpipat.
38		**Chiang Rai, Thailand** — The one place I felt at total peace was Chiang Rai. Less touristy and more open. I had my own little basketed bicycle to explore the area. Just under the main bridge, which was adorned by gilded elephants, sat the opposing simplicities of wood and water.
41		**Bangkok, Thailand** — My last day in Bangkok. Not a city I like to spend much time in, to be honest. But when I asked my hostel host where the old part of the city was, she directed me here. To the "real" market. The market where the Thai locals dance in the glory of fresh produce amid the intense fragrance of seafoods, meats and bright flowers. The deep alleyways; labyrinths of Old Siam.
42		**Bangkok, Thailand** — One of the many *mudras* of the Buddha. I don't actually know the meaning of this *mudra* but I often touch my heart in this way. I believe we are all connected by our hearts. Our hearts contain even more electromagnetic energy than our brains, and brain-like cells have been discovered in our hearts. We not only feel but think with our hearts.
51		**Bangkok, Thailand** — The experience in this temple was one of pure peace. Feminine, in soft pink and gold.

gratitude

This day, my last day in Thailand, I wander aimlessly amongst the Thai and not tourists; absorbing with all of my senses this place that keeps calling to me.

It seems fitting on my last day here that I end my temple experience with death. I want to say by accident but I don't believe there truly are accidents.

I pass by this serene and exquisite *Wat*. Peace and an energy of rest washed over me. I was drawn to enter but sensed this was not a place open to foreigners. As I drank it in from outside, a Thai man, moving boxes in and out for what seemed like some sort of gathering, gestured, asking me if I wanted to enter. I nodded respectfully and he welcomed me in.

Once again, I was overcome by rest, stopped for a place to meditate in a very feminine temple. Soft pinks, golds and flowers ordained this space and I breathed deep.

As I was leaving, an elderly Caucasian man, speaking perfect Thai, was communicating half in Thai and half in English to whom I assumed to be his wife. I heard something about ceremony so I dared softly to ask him what ceremony. At first he seemed a little disgruntled to find me there, not knowing I was invited in, but he indulged my question. His wife's brother recently died and his funeral ceremony was to take place there. He said this was not a temple for tourists so when I realized I was invited earlier, I was honoured.

This *Wat* was a burial place for the Royal Family and related members, of whom his wife was one! He pointed out all of the crypts where the remembered dead laid to rest.

So at the end of my journey here I am reminded of the end of our Journeys Here. Grateful for the blessings of learning. Grateful for the healing of heart. Grateful for the connection of souls and once again reminded to take this home with me. It's easy to get lost in another land but it's even easier to get lost and become unconscious in familiar spaces.

I ask the energies that are greater than me to guide and support this path and to open my heart to love.

Lead with Love.

Thailand, I shall miss you.

(Facebook post from January 20, 2019)

Bangkok, Thailand

the author / photographer

I stand on my head every day and jump out of planes whenever I get the chance.

Viewing the world from a different perspective allows me to see life in a different way.

Although I pursue a career as a food photographer, I have always had an innate knowing that I was supposed to write. In photography school, I was required to take an English Writing class. My instructor asked me to consider writing as my path. Thirty years later, I finally decided to follow that path.

After loss is when the words really start to come. I feel writing doesn't come from me but through me, for when I surrender to what is, the words appear.

Exercise keeps my body and mind healthy. Yoga (including standing on my head) feeds my soul.

I was born and raised in Camrose, Alberta, Canada and currently live in Edmonton, Alberta, Canada.

Sandy Weatherall

Printed in the United States
By Bookmasters